Writing!

Bye, bye writer's block!

5. You're making a YouTube tutorial, but your time limit is 10 minutes. Write a video script so that you sound professional and can fit in all your how-to info.

9. You take part in an experiment where you're frozen and suspended in time for 100 years. What is the world like 100 years on?

14. Write a review of your favourite book.

15. Try writing a story or poem where every sentence has six words or less. Choose a season of the year for the subject.

19. The worst thing that's ever happened to me is...

20. Do a story share with your bestie. Take it in turns to write chapters — just like Ruby and Garnet!

25. Imagine if Beauty moved to Melchester and met Pearl. Choose two characters from different books and bring them together in a new story.

26. What happens next? Pick your favourite JW book and write a sequel!

Turn to the back pages for another six months of writing inspiration!

All About Lily

Age: 9

Birthday: 13 July

Fave JW Book: ....

Fave JW Character: ....

I'm most like: ....

I'm least like: ....

Colour four words that describe you!

Polite Creative

Mischievous Caring

Clever Kind

Arty

Charming Funny

Loud Thoughtful

Sporty Friendly

Calm Quiet

Scientific Chatty

Brave Loyal

Cheeky Quirky

Draw yourself here!

Fave colour: ....

Fave food: ....

Fave movie: ....

Fave YouTuber: ....

I'm good at:

1. ....

2. ....

3. ....

4. ....

5. ....

My happiest memory:

....

....

....

....

My biggest wish: ....

4

Ready, Steady, WRITE!

You too can be an amazing author! Turn over to reveal an exclusive interview with Jacky, read her writing secrets and tips and find answers to all your nosy questions!

Jacky has two books about her own life story, *Jacky Daydream* and *Daydreams and Diaries*. What would you call a book about you?

....

....

....

HETTY Interviews Jacky!

Many people have told me that I'm a one for asking questions. So I shall put that to good use for this interview!

I'm very good at picturing things, but it must take much more than that to write about the past as though you were really there! How do you do it?
I read history books and novels written in late Victorian times — but mostly I try to imagine what it was like. You're very good at that too!

As we all know, Hetty Feather isn't my real name. So how did you think it up? Did you have any other names for me early on?
I decided to give you Hetty as a first name, because it's a typical plain Victorian name — and I gave you Feather as a surname because you are light as a feather.

Jem and Gideon are the dearest boys in the world, each in their own very different ways! Where did you get your inspiration for them?
I thought you needed a very kind patient sweet-tempered older brother who would make you feel special — and I gave you Gideon as a brother because he's delicate and vulnerable and I knew you'd try to look after him.

Which part of my story was your favourite to write about?
I think I enjoyed writing the Tanglefield's Travelling Circus part most. It's so exotic and colourful and I was interested in Madame Adeline.

Which part of my story was the absolute hardest to write?
The hardest part to write was when Matron Bottomly locked you up in the attic — I felt so sorry for you.

If you had a special circus act, what would it be?
I wish I could be a trapeze artist even though I have no head for heights. I suppose the only role I could manage would be the ringmaster — just like you, Hetty.

I hated lots about living at the Foundling Hospital. Which part would you have hated the most?
I'd have hated not being able to curl up in a corner and read a book.

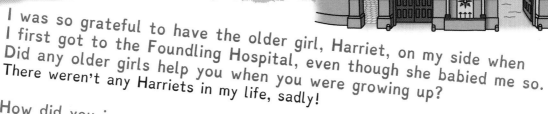

I was so grateful to have the older girl, Harriet, on my side when I first got to the Foundling Hospital, even though she babied me so. Did any older girls help you when you were growing up?
There weren't any Harriets in my life, sadly!

How did you invent such a horrible woman as Matron Stinking Bottomly?
I wanted to write about a really horrible unfair Matron, and yet I tried hard to make her believable too. Maybe I was remembering a few long-ago teachers!

I was absolutely thrilled when Ida gave me a beautiful little copy of *Thumbelina*. What is your most treasured gift?
I'd have liked that little *Thumbelina* book too. I think my most treasured gift has been my beautiful rocking horse. I wish I could let you have a ride on it.

Once, I saw Queen Victoria in a parade to celebrate her Golden Jubilee, though I was quite distracted at the time. Have you ever seen a Queen?
Yes, I've not only seen our current Queen Elizabeth, I've met her several times. I managed a reasonable curtsy. I'd have loved to have met Queen Victoria. Maybe I'll write a future book where you meet royalty too, Hetty.

I always held on to my dreams, even when nobody else believed they could happen. Did you have a dream like that, too?
I've always held onto my dreams too. No one ever believed I'd make it as a writer but I was determined to try. However, you've had a much harder life than me. I wish I had your courage.

If I had been born in your time, how would my story have turned out differently? Is the Foundling Hospital still there?
It moved to different premises in the twentieth century and closed down altogether in the 1950s. If you were born in my time then your mother would have been able to bring you up herself and life would have been so different for both of you.

Are there any other characters from my world that you would love to write about? Perhaps I can let them know!
A girl once emailed me to suggest that I write about Madame Adeline's childhood. I think that's a brilliant idea.

IMAGINE IF...

Matron Wilson ran the Foundling Hospital!

We think the Foundling Hospital would be much better with Matron Wilson in charge! Let's see what she'd change!

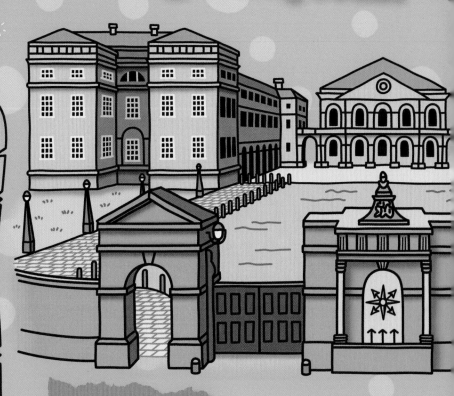

Matron Wilson's Golden Rules!

1. All children to be tucked up in their beds at night and given a cuddly toy.

2. All children should wear soft comfortable clothes, thick coats, scarves and mittens for the winter, and the finest, well-fitting leather shoes.

3. All children should be read to while they do their tasks and allowed to borrow books from the library.

4. All children should go out to play for an hour every day.

What's on the menu?
There will be a varied diet of fresh healthy food — but there'll be a big slice of cake for Sunday tea.

What would Nick's role at the Hospital be?
Nick would be the famous artist who visits once a week to give the children art lessons.

Would you fire any of the Foundling staff from *Hetty Feather*?
Matron Pigface and Matron Bottomly would certainly be sent packing.

Would pets be allowed at the Foundling Hospital?
There would be a special Foundling cat called Thimble and a guard dog (gentle with children) called Growler.

What is absolutely banned at your Foundling Hospital?
There will be no physical punishment whatsoever.

8

Foundling Facts!

The Foundling Hospital was founded by Thomas Coram all the way back in 1739! It was created to care for babies at risk of abandonment.

It was the first children's charity in Britain!

The Foundling Hospital itself might be closed, but the Coram children's charity now helps a million children and young people each year!

The last pupil was placed into foster care in 1954!

Timetable!

Now imagine that YOU run the Hospital! What would a typical day look like?

MORNING

AFTERNOON

EVENING

MENU

_____

_____

_____

_____

_____

LOL with JW!

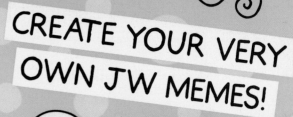

CREATE YOUR VERY OWN JW MEMES!

Cut out and keep!

WHEN YOU UPDATE YOUR FRIENDS ON YOUR LIFE!

NEWS

Walking into the school disco like...

When Dad comes home with Nandos

Write some funny captions of your own!

Smartphone Story Generator

Use your phone to help you write a story!

Amazing Title

What's the name of your fave app or game? This will be your story title and set the tone of your tale. Write it here:

Scene Setter

Open your photo album, close your eyes and count to three. Now point at a photo. What's going on? This will be your story setting.

Main Character

Choose a hero or heroine for your story! Open the contacts list and randomly pick one to be your story star. Write their name here:

Goodies & Baddies

Your story needs some friends and foes!

Use the name of the last person you called to create a story buddy —

The last person you texted will be your evil enemy —

Story Scenario

What's going on in your story? Open the key pad as if you were about to dial a number. Close your eyes and point at the key pad. Match the number you chose to pick a dramatic situation!

1 A beautiful parcel is delivered — but there's nothing to say who's sent it!

2 A note is found inside an old book bought from a slightly strange vintage shop.

3 Your character invents something totally amazing!

4 Someone wins a chance to meet Jacqueline Wilson!

5 Aliens have been spotted playing on the swings in the park. What's going on?

6 Your hero is given a part in a huge Hollywood movie!

7 Bullies are making school miserable for everyone. Who can sort it out?

8 A special lucky charm is lost! Will the luck be lost too?

9 You get a creepy feeling every time you pass a crumbly old house in the street.

0 Uh-oh! There's a BIG falling out between friends.

Twist in the Tale!

Open the camera and hold up your phone. Close your eyes and spin round three times. Keep your eyes closed and snap a photo. What's in the photo? Write it into your story!

Tie Up the End!

Text your bestie and ask her to send you an emoji that describes how she's feeling.

 If you get a happy emoji write a happy ending!

If it's a sad or angry emoji your ending will be a tear jerker.

Ask Jacky ANYTHING!

Get the exclusive answers to YOUR questions!

When you started writing, was there a lot of rejection and how did you deal with it?
Asia-Mae
I certainly had my fair share of rejections. It was always disappointing, but I'd try to work out why to see if there was anything I could change. Sometimes I'd approach a different publisher. I'd try hard not to get too upset.

Would you ever turn one of your books into a movie? If yes, which book would you choose?
Isabel
I'd love lots of my books to be movies, but I'm afraid it's not up to me — it's up to the film production companies! Still, I think *Four Children and It* is going to be made into a movie.

Do you have more plans to include more characters with disabilities in your stories? I'd love to see a character with hearing aids.
Skye
There's an autistic child in *Rose Rivers*, and *Katy* is about a girl coping with a spinal injury. I'll think carefully about a character with hearing aids.

If you were not an author, what would you like to be?
Millie
I'd love to be a bookseller. I often plan in my head how I would run my shop and what the window displays would be like.

What magazines and books did you read when you were younger and did they inspire what you write now?
Katie
I read lots of girls' classics like *Ballet Shoes*, *Little Women*, *What Katy Did* and *A Little Princess*. I also read the *Girl* comic every week, particularly enjoying the true-life stories on the back page.

Would you ever write a story with an animal as the main character?
Jenna
I've actually thought about it, Jenna. My dog Jackson would love to become a literary superstar!

Who would your JW bestie be?

If you could have any friend from all the books you've written, who would it be?
Carly
I think Clover Moon would be a very good friend. Maybe we could make dolls together.

Do you play any musical instruments?
Alyssa
Sadly, I don't play any musical instruments. I learned the recorder at school, but I usually made a terrible squawking noise.

Have you ever met any of your favourite authors? Did they give you any advice?
Emma
The only author I ever met when I was a child was Pamela Brown, who wrote books about children with their own drama company. I was too shy to ask for any advice.

What character is most similar to the way you were as a child?
Erin
I think I was a mixture of the twins in *Double Act*, Ruby and Garnet. I was usually quiet and shy and imaginative like Garnet, but I rather liked standing on a stage like Ruby.

Which character are you like?

STORY VIBES BOARD!

Make a writer's mood board to inspire you!

Use your writer's mood board to collect images and text to help you see what your next story will be like! You can stick up photos of people to be your next main character, photos of interesting places to use as your next setting and words that capture your theme! Add JW quotes to keep up your motivation!

YOU'LL NEED:

- ⭐ Canvas
- ⭐ Foam or wadding
- ⭐ Fabric
- ⭐ Ribbon
- ⭐ Strong glue
- ⭐ Drawing pins
- ⭐ Split pins
- ⭐ Scissors
- ⭐ Ruler

Ask an adult to help you!

1. Cut the foam or wadding to size and stick it on your canvas with strong glue. Leave to dry and trim off the edges.

2. Canvas-side down, measure and cut a piece of fabric allowing an extra 8cm on each side.

3. Fold each corner of the fabric down, then pin them in place with drawing pins, like this!

4. Fold down the length of the fabric, tuck it in and pin into place. Make sure it's pulled tight!

5. Cut lengths of ribbon to go diagonally across the board. Add an extra 3cm to each end and use drawing pins to pin them in place at the back. Start with an X and keep adding them diagonally, like this!

6. Use a sharp pencil to poke holes where the ribbons cross, then push the split pins through.

Can you guess which JW book this mood board might have inspired?

Answer: Rent a Bridesmaid

17

HELLO, AMAZING AUTHOR!

Follow my ultimate writing tips and watch your stories start to flow!

1. Read Lots!

This isn't to copy other people's ideas, it's to increase your vocabulary and stimulate your imagination. It will also help you learn punctuation and grammar without too much strain.

2. Keep a Daily Diary

It will get you into a regular writing habit. So many people want to write but never settle down and actually do so.

3. Think Hard About Your Characters

What do they look like, what do they love doing, what frightens them, what do they secretly wish for? Get to know them well before you start writing!

4. Choose a Setting You Find Interesting

It could be a bustling town or a tiny country village or a seaside resort, but try to make it seem real — even if it's a fairy tale palace in a fantasy.

5. When is Your Story Set?

Past or present, maybe World War Two, or Victorian times? Take care not to make basic mistakes like having historical children using mobiles or tablets! Perhaps you'd like to write about the future?

6. First Person or Third?

Are you going to write in the first person, with the main character telling the story, or in the third person, when you write the story yourself and tell us what the characters are doing? Either way is fine, whichever is easiest for you.

7. What Type of Story Should You Write?

Funny or sad, a gentle family story or a thriller with lots of action? Is it going to be a really long story that lasts for many pages, or is it going to be short and sweet? Pace your story accordingly.

8. Something Has to Happen!

In all stories, there has to be some conflict, a problem your character has to solve in some way. Don't try to work it all out at once — ideas can pop up when you're right in the middle of writing.

9. Don't Stress Over the Start!

It's great to have an eye-catching beginning, but don't agonise over this too much or you'll never get started! You can always go back and rewrite passages that aren't working to improve your story.

10. A Final Flourish!

Will you finish with everything ending happily ever after, or choose a sad story to make everyone cry? Nothing is more satisfying than writing those magic words THE END at the bottom of the page!

WHO'S WHO

Write character profiles before you start. Add lots of detail about their looks and personality, then refer to your notes to keep everything correct when you write your story. Here's a game to help you —

WHAT TO DO:

- Write the numbers 1 to 6 and the letters A to F on separate scraps of paper. Pop them in two bowls.
- Pick a number and match it to the list below to find a character.
- Pick a letter to reveal something to add to their description.

Make up new suggestions of your own — try some animal characters!

1. An obnoxious girl who always gets her own way.

2. A lady who once was a big theatre star.

3. A shy boy who is part of a big, rowdy family.

4. A teacher who is very, very strict.

5. A shopkeeper who sells the most unusual objects.

6. A parent who has a sad secret.

A. The cleverest person you've ever met.

B. Has a hidden talent for being a brilliant baker.

C. Wears the same cardigan every day — just like Dixie Diamond!

D. Likes to try out odd hair colours and styles.

Play again and again for different outcomes!

E. Is a champion swimmer.

F. Worries about absolutely everything.

DO IT!

Try my challenges to get started!

Picture It! ☆ ☆

If you find diary writing hard, do a picture journal. Doodle something that happened or take a photo and write a short description. Now use your visuals for story inspiration! Try a sketch or stick a photo here –

Book Bling-up!

Make a basic description sound super-interesting! Embellish these sentences, I've helped out with the first one –

1 The car was blue.

> The famous footballer's car was a glittering turquoise blue – almost as dazzling as his swimming pool.

2 She found herself in a room.

3 Suddenly, the lights went out.

4 It was cold and lonely.

5 A boy stood before them.

Big Read!

Read at least one chapter of a book every day for a week!

Tick off the days

Mon ☐	**Tues** ☐
Wed ☐	**Thurs** ☐
Fri ☐	**Sat** ☐
Sun ☐	

WELL DONE!

So Many Words!

Sometimes all you need to transform a story is to use new words. Simply replacing the word 'said' with another choice can make a big difference. Here are some others you can pick – try it and see what happens!

Grumbled · Insisted · Smirked · Cried · Gulped · Yelled · Shouted · Joked · Whispered · Giggled · Muttered · Gasped · Whined · Begged · Sang

Can you think of any more?

Let's DIY!

Show off your DIY skills and create marvellous makes! You can do it!

Stick a picture of something you've made here!

Organise Your Writer's Toolbox!

You'll Need:

- ★ A box
- ☆ Card
- ☆ Ruler
- ★ Scissors
- ☆ Glue

1. Measure the depth, length and width of the inside of your box.

2. Cut out a piece of card that is double the depth of the box and add 2 cm to the length or width.

3. Fold the card in half so it's the depth of the box.

4. Measure 1 cm in from each end and make a mark. Cut along the folded crease up to the mark, then fold the ends out to make a flat end you can glue to the inside of your box. Glue the card shut and stick into your box, like this!

5. Add as many sections as you want! Remember to keep measuring with each new section you add!

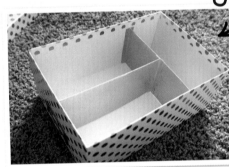

JW Pen Pots!

You'll Need:

- ☆ Jars
- ★ Card
- ☆ Glue
- ☆ Washi tape
- ★ Character cut-outs from page 91

1. Measure the height of your jar and cut a piece of card — make it long enough to wrap right round.

Writing Desk!

JW pens and pencils — you can never have too many writing utensils!

A notepad and fave pen!

Fill a section with story starters! Fold them up and pick them out when you need an inspiration boost!

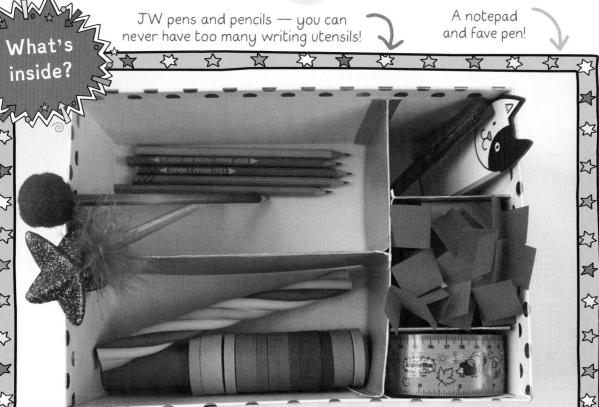

Washi tape and a giant JW eraser!

A JW roll-up ruler!

2. Use washi tape to make cute patterns on your card and add your character cut-outs.

3. Wrap the card around your jar and glue it down at the back where it overlaps!

DAISY'S DESIGN STUDIO!

Find out how to do this pretty nail art, then create your own design!

You'll Need:

- ☆ Green polish
- ★ White polish
- ☆ Yellow polish
- ☆ Foil nail strips
- ★ Toothpick
- ☆ Thin paintbrush

1. Start by painting two of your nails green, and paint your pointer finger, thumb and your pinky white.

2. Use a thin paintbrush to gently paint on some daisy petals in white polish.

3. Dot on some yellow polish using a toothpick for the centres. Once it's dry, lay the nail foil strips vertically on your pointer, thumb and pinky nails.

4. Paint over the top using the green, so that when you peel it away, white lines are left. Cover in a clear top coat once it's dry to seal it all in.

WHY NOT?

Try doing three dotty nails instead of stripes.

YouTube/CutePolish

BUILD A B

You'll Need:

⭐ Oven bake craft clay – we used Fimo Soft

⭐ Wooden cocktail sticks

Follow the diagram to roll and shape all the parts of the bunny's body.

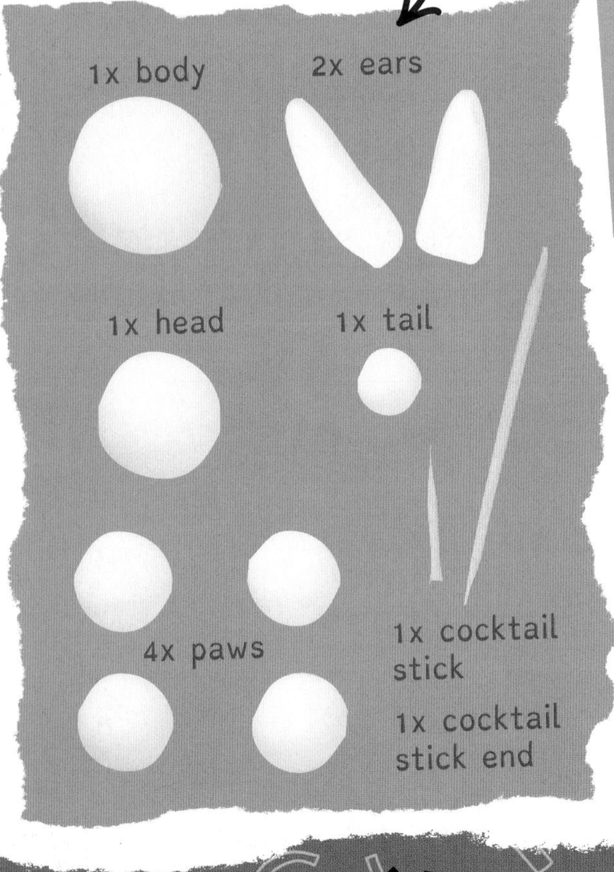

1. Flatten the narrow ends of the paws a little by gently pressing with your thumb. Make the two front paws slightly longer.

2. Cut the end off a cocktail stick and use it to fasten the head to the body. Press the tail and front and back paws on to the bunny body.

3. Add the ears next. Gently press each one against the sides of the head.

1x body

2x ears

1x head

1x tail

4x paws

1x cocktail stick

1x cocktail stick end

Your bunny can be any colour you like!

UNNY

I'll show you how!

4. Roll two small balls of black clay for the eyes, and a little triangle of pink for the nose.

5. Use a cocktail stick to prick some whisker holes and a little mouth.

Ask an adult to help you cut the cocktail sticks!

Now follow the instructions on the clay pack to bake your cute little critter. Ask an adult to help with the oven.

EVERYTHING
BASIC BUNTING!

Transform your paper scraps into lovely room decorations.

1. Use the bunting template from page 93. Draw round it then cut lots of diamonds from your paper scraps. Fold each one in half to make triangles.

2. Sandwich your string inside the paper triangles and stick the two sides together with glue or double-sided sticky tape.

3. Keep adding bunting shapes till you have a long garland like this.

You'll Need:

★ Scrap paper
☆ String
★ Double-sided sticky tape or glue

BUTTERFLY GARLAND

You'll Need:

★ String
★ Hole punch
☆ Scrap card and paper

My string of butterflies is perfect for a summer den.

1. Use the butterfly template from page 93. Draw round it and cut lots of butterflies from your scraps.

2. Punch a hole at the tip of each top wing like this

BUNTING!

TEENY TINY BUNTING!

You'll Need:
- ⭐ Paper scraps
- ⭐ String
- ⭐ Double-sided sticky tape

1. Start by making some craft tape. Turn your paper so the wrong side is facing up. Cut a length of double-sided sticky tape and stick it to the paper like this.

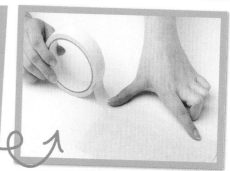

2. Carefully trim round the edge of the tape like this. Don't peel off the tape backing just yet, cut your tape into little tabs around 3 — 5cm long and fold in half.

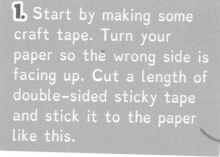

3. Peel off the backing tape, sandwich some string between the folded tabs and stick together.

4. Now just trim the tabs into bunting and flag shapes like this.

Use your tiny bunting to decorate pin boards, bookshelves and pen pots!

3. Copy the picture and thread the string through the holes to create a gorgeous garland of fluttery butterflies!

Brilliant for your bedroom!

DIY Unicorn Book Marks

These mystical creatures are galloping to keep your page!

You'll need:

☆ SCRAP PAPER
★ GLUE STICK
☆ PEN

Turn to **page 89** and cut out the paper strips, ear and unicorn horn. Or use your own paper scraps — start with a **rectangle 10cm wide and 19cm long.**

① Make the head from the large paper strip. With any design to the outside, start by folding in half lengthwise.

② Fold in half width ways to mark the centre line and open up again. Starting with the crease to the bottom, fold one side in to meet the centre line like this.

③ Repeat on the other side so both ends are folded up.

④ Flip over to the other side. Fold the top tabs down to meet the paper edge like this.

⑤ Now copy the picture to fold down the four corners and create a heart shape. Glue down these little tabs.

Let's Decorate!

① Glue the ear under the centre flap at the point of the heart. Now glue down the front flaps of the heart.

② Glue the mane strip along the back of the head. Snip off the extra and glue it to the front. Cut into fringes.

③ Finish by drawing on the eye and nostril and gluing on the horn. Why not add some glitter too?

Slip the little pocket over the corner of your page!

SLIME IN [

Molten Metallic

You'll Need:

☆ PVA glue
★ Contact lens solution
☆ Metallic read[
    mix paint
★ Glitter paint
☆ Bicarbonate c
    soda
★ Plastic bowl

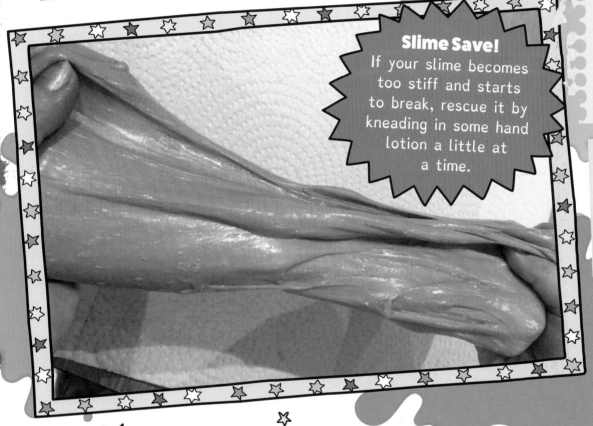

Slime Save!
If your slime becomes too stiff and starts to break, rescue it by kneading in some hand lotion a little at a time.

1. Put 120ml of PVA glue in the bowl, add a squirt of metalli[paint and mix together.

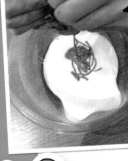

Snow Fluff Slime

You'll Need:

☆ PVA glue
★ Contact lens solution
☆ White or silver glitter
★ Bicarbonate of soda
☆ Plastic bowl
★ Shaving foam

1. Start as before with the glue, and bicarbonate of soda. Gently stir in 1¼ cups of shaving foam, then slowly mix in the contact lens solution.

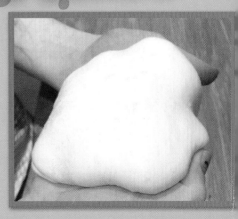

10 TIME!

Follow these recipes for a super slime-fest!

1. The contact lens solution is the slime activator. Check the ingredients to make sure it contains *boric acid*, *sodium borate*, or both.

3. Start to add the contact lens solution one teaspoon at a time — you shouldn't need any more than 4 – 6 teaspoons in total.

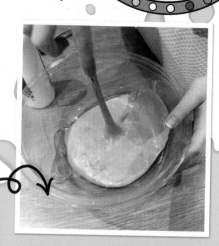

4. The slime should begin to get stretchy and gloopy like this. Take your time and keep stirring!

5. When it's thicker like this, it's time for kneading. Use a plastic tray, or cover the surface with cling film first.

2. Now add in a blob of glitter paint for some sparkle, then stir in 1 teaspoon of bicarbonate of soda.

6. Fold, knead and prod your slime till any slippery residue disappears.

7. It's ready when it no longer sticks to your hands and is stretchy and squishy!

2. Knead in the glitter – this slime should be fluffy like marshmallow. Add more shaving foam if you need more fluff.

3. When it's ready, fluffy slime should keep a shape for a little while. Twist it and swirl it around like an ice cream to check!

Pink Menace Bubblegum Slime

1. Start with the glue, bicarbonate of soda and paint as before, plus a big squirt of shaving foam (about a cupful).

2. Gently stir everything together then start to add the contact lens solution.

3. When it's ready to knead, sprinkle over the glitter powder and work it in as you go. It's ready when it's stretchy and no longer sticky.

You'll Need:

Ingredients as before, but:

☆ Swap the metallic paint for neon paint

★ Swap the glitter paint for glitter powder

☆ You'll also need a tin of shaving foam

Bubblicious!
Make a giant bubble! Hold up your slime and let it droop and stretch out really thinly, then quickly flip down on to the surface. Keep trying till you get a big bubble like this!

Draw and Design!

Ooh, there are so many art secrets to be revealed! Sneak a peek at Nick Sharratt's studio and find out what he gets up to all day!

Sketch your self-portrait here!

Let's Get ARTY!

Nick Sharratt answers our burning questions!

If you could swap jobs with anyone, who would you swap with?

I wouldn't mind swapping jobs with the illustrator Axel Scheffler and then I could say, 'Yes, I drew the Gruffalo.' It's extraordinary how often I get asked by little children if I did!

THE GRUFFALO

What's the hardest thing in the world to draw?

For me, personally, a really convincing hamster or gerbil!

Who's your biggest arty inspiration?

A wonderful artist called Tony Hart who was on television when I was a boy. He inspired many, many children, including me, to try out different kinds of art for themselves.

Who do you prefer: Tracy Beaker or Hetty Feather?

For illustrating, Tracy Beaker, as I love doing her hair. I'm not so fond of drawing Hetty's braids!

If you could buy any piece of art in the world, what would it be?

A large sculpture by the artist Barbara Hepworth!

If you could have tea with one person from the past, who would it be and why?

I'd have tea outdoors with one of the French Impressionist painters. It would be warm and sunny; the setting would be beautiful and I just know the food would be delicious!

If you could only draw one thing for the rest of your life, what would it be?

Cats!

Jacqueline Wilson
The Story of Tracy Beaker
Illustrated by Nick Sharratt

How did you become an illustrator?

I did as much art as I possibly could at school and at home, then I got a place at art college to learn how to become a professional illustrator. After that I went to lots and lots of publishers of books and magazines with my drawings in the hope that they would commission me to do illustrations for them — and thankfully some of them did!

Which arty style is your absolute favourite?

I really like pop art!

ZAP!

Sketch Secrets!

Want to be an illustrator like Nick? Just follow his top tips!

1. To improve your drawing skills, do plenty of sketching from real life.

2. Try to finish your pictures if you can — don't give up halfway.

3. Be patient! Don't rush things if you have a large space to colour in, or something that needs to be filled with a fiddly pattern.

4. If you do make a mistake you can't rub out, cover it up with a carefully cut-out and glued-down patch of paper, and continue drawing on top. It's what professional illustrators do!

5. Keep a sketch book with you, for making quick sketches of interesting people, places or things, and jotting down any ideas for pictures that might occur to you.

Draw It!

☆ Today, I saw:

Nick's Studio Sneak

My studio secrets revealed!

I need lots of book shelves in my studio, especially for all the Jacqueline Wilson books. Sometimes, I feel a bit like a librarian, trying to keep them in some kind of order.

I'm running out of space for all of Jacqueline's books!

I keep my pens and pencils in special mugs.

Arts & Crafts!

In my plan chest, I have drawers for artwork, posters and different kinds of drawing paper.

Fan Mail!

It's lovely to receive letters and brilliant drawings from fans!

I sometimes use paint to colour my pictures but more often I use my computer.

Rose Rivers Roughs!

I have to do lots of sketches before I get my illustrations how I want them. These are some preparatory drawings of Rose Rivers!

Sneaky peek sketches!

Peek!

My Messy Desk!

As you can see from my desk, I'm not very tidy!

I'm never short of notebooks. Lots of them have come from Jacqueline Wilson Magazine!

We ♥ Nick's posters!

Even my mouse mat has Jacqueline Wilson characters on it!

Jolly files make doing all the boring administrative type jobs a bit more fun!

Recognise any of these characters?

My Top Tools!

I couldn't work without...

A pad of layout paper — ideal for rough drawings as it's just thin enough for tracing when I'm reworking sketches.

A pad of cartridge paper — for doing my final line drawings on. It has a very slightly textured surface.

Soft pencils, between 3B and 6B — so much easier to draw with than a hard H pencil!

Masking tape — for holding drawings in place when tracing. I get through rolls and rolls of the stuff!

Putty rubber — it's much gentler on paper than one of those hard, scratchy erasers.

Slippers — I can't work if my feet are cold. These are my current slippers!

The one on the right is my favourite!

A DAY IN THE LIFE OF

Lily watson

Add your name!

Now complete your day diary!

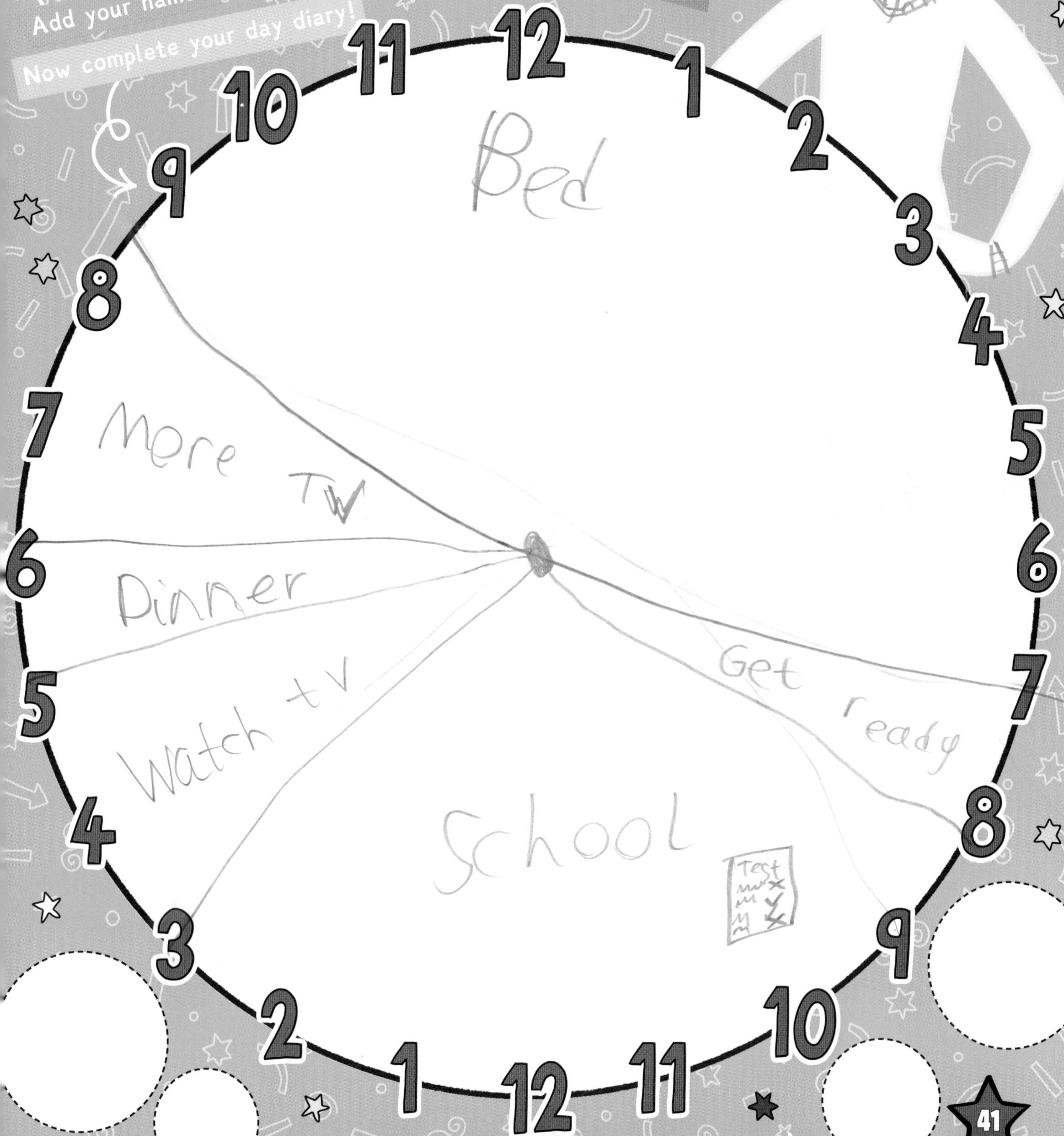

Draw yourself here!

12 1 2 3 4 5 6 7 8 9 10 11 12 1 2 3 4 5 6 7 8 9 10 11

Bed

More TV

Dinner

Watch tv

School

Get ready

Test

41

Sketch some details from your day!

DOODLE YOUR LIFE!

Take our daily doodle challenge!

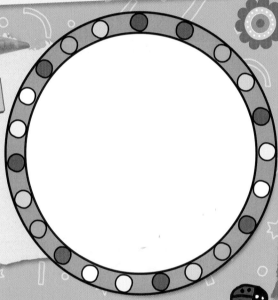

Motivational Monday!

Draw a portrait of somebody you really admired today.

Weird Wednesday!

ONLY use random shapes and colours to describe how you felt today.

Terrific Tuesday!

Make a collage of all the things you loved about today.

Use these prompts to start your scrapbook!

Thrilling Thursday!

Doodle something from your day without ever lifting your pen off the page.

Friendship Friday!

Make a cute collage for your BFF using magazines, newspapers and scraps.

Silly Saturday!

Keep your camera at the ready to snap something LOL-worthy today.

Stick your photo here!

Why not?

Keep going! Try to doodle, draw, snap or scrapbook something each day all month or even all year!

Sunday Fun Day!

Create your dream day out by doodling, photo-taking and scrapbooking!

SCRAP BOOK

Rose an[d]

Pencils at the ready!

Rose Rivers

1. Draw a U shape for Rose's face, with two round ears. Add lines for her neck, the top shape of her dress and a curvy collar.

2. Sketch in hair around her face, gathering at the back. Add frills to her dress, and two billowing sleeves, with slimmer arms at the bottom.

3. Finish off the outline of Rose's dress, then add a V shaped bodice and frilly cuffs to her sleeves. Draw lines for her fringe, with one loose hair escaping.

4. Sketch a bow, then add lots of lines to her hair. Draw one hand, with her finger pointing down, then draw in her other hand, slightly behind the first one. Add more details to the dress and give her curved boots.

5. Finish off her boots with buttons, a sole and a line down the middle. Add the details of her face, then colour her in!

Why not pick your own favourite colours for Rose's dress?

d Clover!

Clover Moon

Here's how to draw Clover as a nursery maid!

1. Give Clover a wobbly U-shaped face. Draw wavy lines for her hair and curves for her ears. Add a neck, frilly collar and V shape for the top of her uniform.

2. Add two lines around the V shape to make it thicker, then a chunky band along the middle. Give her short, frilly shoulders. Add a cap on her head.

3. Draw a curvy line for the top of her pinafore and two lines for the top of her body. Now give her two long arms, cuffs on her sleeves and hands.

4. Dot a design onto the top of her collar and pinafore, then draw the outline of her pinafore and dress underneath. Sketch in the top of her boots. Add wispy bits of messy hair around her head and draw in the details of her face. Add lines to her pinafore and finish off her boots.

5. Decorate the pinafore with more lines and dots, then add laces to the boots. Colour in the finished picture — don't forget to give her rosy cheeks!

Design & Colour Poster!

Make a wish and colour this poster your way!

Cut out and keep!

Wishes come true!

100% Cringe!

What's your biggest cringe moment? Reveal it here:

....
....
....
....
....
....

So many blushes and LOLs! You'll be 100%

Blush-a-rama Drama!

Pick a character, then write a totally cringe-worthy story!

What to do!

Tick four statements to find out which character to use for your story, then find your plot on the other page!

I turn my cringing situations into hilarious comedy material! ☐

There's nothing better than curling up with a good book. ☐

I'm really close to my siblings. ☐

Confidence is my middle name! ☐

I'm super-clumsy. ☐

I like to make a fashion statement! ☐

I love adventure! ☐

I love making different concoctions in the kitchen. ☐

I've read over 100 books! ☐

Pizza is my fave food. ☐

I love playing pranks! ☐

I try to keep my cool at all times. ☐

Your cringe character is...

Mostly blue... Tracy!

Mostly pink... Ruby!

Mostly purple... Jacky!

Now pick your embarrassing situation!

Write about a time when your character embarrasses themselves on stage in front of a full audience of friends and family — like Garnet in the nativity scene in *Double Act*!

Your character gets into an argument with someone in the school lunch hall, and a *huge* food fight breaks out. Suddenly, a big ball of spaghetti is hurtling toward them — what happens next?!

Your character gets surprise-attacked by her awful sister and silly BFF — right before she's about to go out with her friends! Now your character is covered in egg and her friends are at the door...

WARNING: Major cringes ahead!

Use the space below to jot down some notes about your character and a rough beginning, middle and end for your plot!

My character is:

....

Character traits:

....

....

Beginning:

....

....

....

Middle:

....

....

Ending:

....

....

....

Time to write your story

_____

_____

_____

_____

_____

_____

_____

_____

_____

_____

_____

_____

_____

_____

_____

_____

_____

_____

SLEEPOVER

HOW TO PLAY

1. Take turns throwing a dice and move around the board, following the instructions.

2. Use buttons as counters.

3. If you land on a DARE box, spin the dial below and take up the challenge to move ahead — go back to the start if you fail!

4. The first player to reach the end wins!

Dare Dial

Swap socks with the person on your left.

Eat a spoonful of mustard with pepper sprinkled on top. Blurgh!

Name 10 animals that begin with the letter C.

Mime an animal. If no one guesses what it is, spin again!

Stuff marshmallows in your mouth and sing Happy Birthday.

Give the person on your left a piggyback ride around the room.

Lip-sync along to a song of your friend's choosing.

Get a silly makeover, take a selfie and send it to all your contacts.

Wrap yourself in toilet paper and parade around the house.

Share an embarrassing secret that no one else knows.

Put a pencil in the middle and give it a spin — if you dare!

SPIN IT!

Who'll be crowned the sleepover queen? Play along to find out!

START

1  Amy

2 You get a glam makeover — skip ahead two spaces!

3 DARE

4  Bella

DARE

16

5 You've dropped the popcorn. Miss a turn picking it up.

 Roll a six to move ahead.

6  POP CORN

WINNER!

 Emily

7  Chloe

DARE

11  Daisy

10 DARE

9 You confess your biggest secret — eek! Head back to 4.

8 DARE

TOTALLY TRUE CONFESSIONS!

Now it's time to reveal your darkest secrets — no fibbing!

Ok, I admit I may have (I repeat, may have) accidentally (on purpose) broken Justine-Annoying-Wretch-Littlewood's precious Mickey Mouse clock...

Justine asks...

Have you ever broken something precious then said 'it wasn't me'?

YES ☐   NO ☐

Elaine The Pain asks...

Have you ever skipped school?

YES ☐   NO ☐

Louise asks...

Have you been mean to a friend?

YES ☐   NO ☐

Peter asks...

Have you been mean to a friend then not apologised afterwards?

YES ☐   NO ☐

Miss Brown asks...

Have you made up an elaborate excuse for not doing your homework?

YES ☐   NO ☐

Football asks...

Ever done a dare you knew was Extremely Dangerous?

YES ☐   NO ☐

CAN YOU HANDLE THE CRINGE?

Welcome to the ULTIMATE JW cringe quiz!

Add up your points as you go to reveal your results on the JW Cringe-o-Meter!

START
You're a star performer!

Show your baby photos? NEVER! — NO

Seat at the back of the class, please! — YES

You always just say what you're thinking!

You LOVE practical jokes!

You don't blush, you go BEETROOT red!

YES / NO / YES / NO / YES / NO / YES

Cool and collected — 5 Points
You're not fazed by anything, are you?

Rosy Glow — 10 Points
Some things can be embarrassing, but you love a joke!

Big Blusher — 15 Points
The slightest thing will make your cheeks turn bright red!

Have you ever...

Tick every box that applies to you! Each box is worth three points!

- ☐ Fallen over in front of your crush?
- ☐ Sneezed really loud during a school assembly?
- ☐ Sung a song super-loud and not realised?
- ☐ Been caught dancing by yourself?
- ☐ Been hit by a snowball in the playground?
- ☐ Said something REALLY embarrassing?
- ☐ Not realised you had food on your face?
- ☐ Been splashed by a passing car?
- ☐ Accidentally left your diary open?
- ☐ Worn a crazy jumper your nan knitted for you?

This or That!

Challenge time! You HAVE to pick one of the outcomes below. The green text is worth ONE point, and the red text is worth TWO points!

Sing in the school choir...
OR
Sing a solo?

Read aloud in class...
OR
Be the lead part in the school play?

Bring your dad to school...
OR
Have your dad as your teacher?

Go to a fancy dress party as a group...
OR
Go in your own eye-catching attire?

Show ONE person a silly selfie...
OR
Have a silly selfie made into a poster?

Trip over a shoe lace...
OR
Be splashed by a puddle?

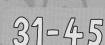

46-57
You are QUEEN of cringe! The slightest thing will turn your cheeks red — and that's okay!

31-45
You're no stranger to blushing, but you handle it like a pro! You still love to be super-silly!

11-30
You're totally cool — and don't embarrass easily! You're super confident and we think that's awesome!

Now it's time to add up all of your points!

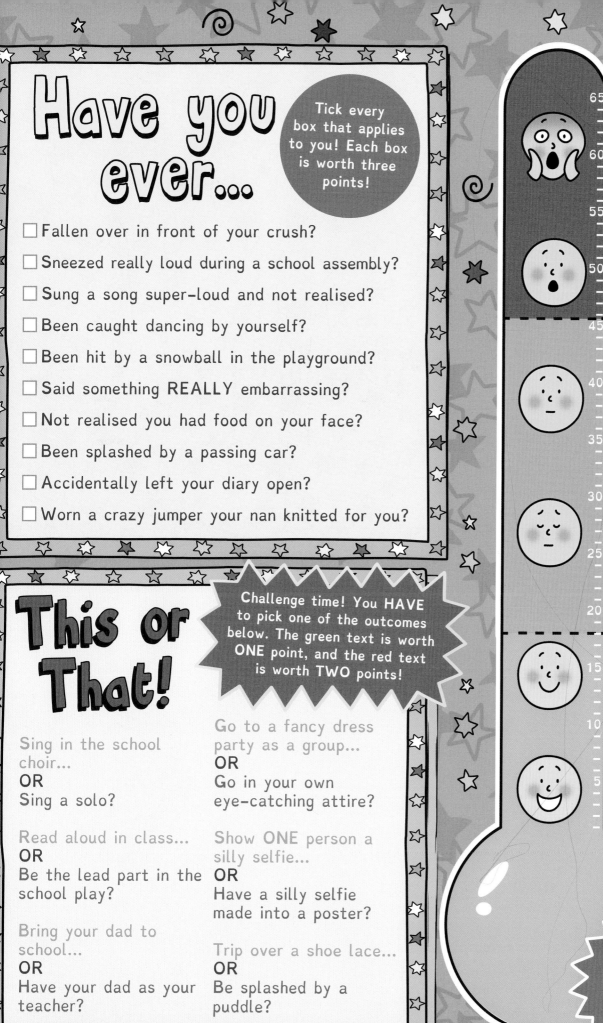

Sunset and Destiny's Shuffle Game!

Play our shuffle cringe game if you dare!

HOW TO PLAY:
Recruit your friends to play with, pick a playlist and hit shuffle. Each new song decides the fate of each person — take it in turns!

Round 1: Title Truths!

If the title has any of the words to the right, tell the truth! If the title doesn't have any of the words, then you're safe till your next go! If it has more than one, your friends get to choose for you! Have one go each.

Girl – What's your biggest wish?
Never – Make up a question for somebody else!
Love – Who's your latest celebrity crush?
Rock – What was your most embarrassing moment?
Heart – Give a compliment to each of your friends!
Beautiful – What do you love that everyone else hates?
Together – Tell your friends a secret!

Round 2: Dance Dares!

Spin a pencil on the wheel to find out what kind of dance to do to the music! Have a go each!

Dance Dares!
Ballet
Tap
Flamenco
Waltz
Disco
Robot

Round 3: Musical Mayhem!

Play this round three times each. Use the first letter of the first song title to find your dare below. For the second song, use the last letter of the title and for the third song, use the first letter of the artist or group. Take it in turns with your friends!

A – Shout out the chorus as loud as you can!
B – Do a silly dance
C – Try to sing the lyrics backwards!
D – Do an impression of your fave singer
E – What would your band name be?
F – Sing the song while holding your nose!
G – Sing the rest of the song like a sheep!
H – Dance like a chicken!
I – Make the song operatic
J – Dress up like your fave singer
K – Make up your own song!
L – Sign an autograph
M – Play air guitar!
N – Ballroom dance with the person to your left
O – Be a ballerina
P – Squeak the song like a mouse!
Q – Play musical bumps for the rest of the song!
R – Sing the song reeeally slowly
S – Sing the song super-fast!
T – Tweet the song like a bird
U – Sing the song as a cartoon character
V – Mime the words and give it your all
W – Pretend to be a DJ
X – Squeeze your cheeks together and try to sing
Y – Whisper the rest of the song
Z – Hum the song as loud as you can

Worry Website to the Rescue!

Our tips can help beat your blushes!

"I'm no good at making new friends!"

"Who'd want to talk to me? I'm boring!"

"I never know what to say to people."

"I'm scared to go somewhere new in case I make a fool of myself."

"My shyness stops me doing things I'd really like to do."

"I hate going somewhere if I don't know anyone!"

Do you ever have these thoughts? Don't worry, most people have the same fears!

Relax!

Going into a new situation can make you feel anxious and tongue-tied. Sort out your shyness by focussing on other things.

⭐ Imagine going somewhere and having a great time. Picture what it will be like to have lots of fun.

⭐ Play some of your favourite tunes and dance around while you get ready to take your mind off your worries.

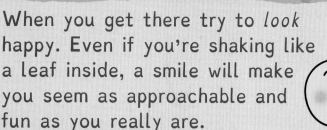

Smile!

When you get there try to *look* happy. Even if you're shaking like a leaf inside, a smile will make you seem as approachable and fun as you really are.

Questions!

Take the attention away from you by concentrating on others and asking questions. Practise saying your questions with a smile before you go out.

Here are some ideas –

- ☆ Where do you go to school?
- ☆ What subjects do you like best?
- ☆ Do you like JW books? Which is your fave?
- ☆ What TV shows do you watch?
- ☆ What singers or bands do you like?
- ☆ What hobbies do you have?

Keep your own answers simple until your confidence builds up.

For example, say something like "Oh, I love *Cookie* too. What was your fave part of the book?" This keeps the focus on the other person and not on you.

Try to remember the answers and use them later. This will make you a great person to talk to.

Sooo Embarrassed!

If you feel yourself start to blush, be honest and laugh. Just say "I feel so nervous, I can't believe my face is like a tomato!"

Everyone blushes or feels awkward and shy at some point so no one will think you're silly. They probably feel the same.

YUM, YUM, YUM!

Let's get cooking in the kitchen! Treat your friends and family to some tasty goodies.

What's your best show stopping bake? Draw a picture of it here!

Madame Adeline's Circus Pony Cake!

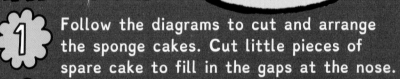

Make a cake that looks just like Pirate!

You'll Need:

- 2 round sponge cakes — use Hetty's recipe or buy ready made
- 100g butter or margarine
- 200g icing sugar
- 1 tablespoon cocoa powder
- Rainbow laces or fruit strips
- Sweets and feathers to decorate

WHAT TO DO:

1 Follow the diagrams to cut and arrange the sponge cakes. Cut little pieces of spare cake to fill in the gaps at the nose.

2 For icing, beat the butter and sugar together until soft and smooth.

3 Take out one large spoonful of the icing and mix the cocoa powder into this.

4 Cover the cakes with the plain icing. Add Pirate's eye patch with chocolate icing round the eye area.

Always ask and adult before using any kitchen equipment.

How to divide up your cake!

ear | spare
spare | nose
ear

Now copy the picture to decorate — here's what you'll need:

Mane:
rainbow laces or fruit strips

Eyelashes:
cut small pieces of liquorice or rainbow laces

Eye:
a Malteser

Finish with some fancy trims — we placed on a flower brooch for effect.

Hetty's Very Victorian Victoria Sponge!

WHAT TO DO:

1. Preheat the oven to 180C/350F/Gas 4. Grease and line 2 x 20cm sandwich tins.

2. Break the eggs into a large mixing bowl, then add the sugar, flour, baking powder and butter in that order.

3. Use a hand mixer or wooden spoon to mix together until well combined — be careful not to over mix.

4. Divide the mixture evenly between the tins and bake in the centre of the oven for 20-25 minutes.

5. The cakes are done when they're golden-brown and spring back when you gently press the tops. Leave to cool in the tins for five minutes, then turn onto a wire cooling rack to cool completely.

You'll Need:
- 4 eggs
- 225g caster sugar
- 225g self-raising flour
- 2tsp baking power
- 225g soft butter or margarine

Read about Madame Adeline and Pirate in *Hetty Feather*!

Try my easy all-in-one recipe!

FRUITY SNACKS!

These snacks might be healthy — but they taste SO good!

Remember, always ask an adult to help in the kitchen!

Strawberry Smoothie!

You'll need:

Serves 2!

- ✔ 8 strawberries
- ✔ 110ml skimmed milk
- ✔ 120g low fat plain yoghurt
- ✔ 3 tablespoons of demerara sugar
- ✔ 1 teaspoon of vanilla extract
- ✔ 6 crushed ice cubes

① Chop up the strawberries and set them to one side. Measure up the rest of your ingredients.

② Add all of your ingredients to a food blender. Blend everything together until it looks nice and smooth.

Top Tip! Stir the mixture through to find any lumps!

③ Carefully pour the smoothie into two tall glasses. Add a pretty straw to each and share with a friend — yummy!

Serves 6!

Fruity Pops!

You'll need:

✔ 16 large strawberries
✔ A mango
✔ 4 kiwis
✔ Water for blending
✔ Ice pop mould

1 Blend all of your fruit down separately. Start with the strawberries by popping them in a food blender and blending until smooth.

2 Repeat step one with the mangos and kiwis separately. Add a little water to make it extra smooth!

3 Pour a little of the strawberry mixture into the ice pop moulds. Put it in the freezer for 25 minutes. Once frozen, add the mango mixture and freeze again for 25 minutes. Repeat with the kiwi mixture and put back in the freezer for another 25 minutes.

4 Once your ice pops have frozen, gently ease them out and share with your BFFs. Quick — before they melt!

How to Make Your Own Pizza

Fast 'n' Fresh Pizza Dough

Make a tasty pizza from scratch. I'll show you how!

You'll need:

- ⭐ 1 cup of self-raising flour
- ⭐ 1 cup of Greek yogurt
- ⭐ Pinch of salt

Use a small tea cup if you don't have measuring cups!

① Put all the ingredients into a bowl and use a spoon to start stirring it all together.

② When the mix begins to stick, knead it together by hand to make a dough ball like this.

③ Cover a baking tray with foil and brush on a little olive oil. Now use your fingers to press the dough flat, making a big, thin circle. Prick with a fork.

Super-Healthy Sauce!

You'll need:
- ⭐ Tin of tomatoes
- ⭐ 1 dessert spoon of tomato puree
- ⭐ ½ chopped onion
- ⭐ 1 chopped garlic clove
- ⭐ 2 small grated carrots
- ⭐ Pinch of salt and pepper
- ⭐ ½ tsp sugar
- ⭐ 2 tsp oil for frying

Ask an adult to help with this!

1 Heat the oil in a pan and add the onion and garlic. Fry until soft — if the pan gets too dry, add a little splash of water.

2 Add all the other ingredients and stir together. When the mix starts to bubble, turn down the heat.

3 Let the sauce mix simmer, stirring occasionally. Once it's nice and thick, leave to cool for 10 minutes. Now spread it on your pizza base like this.

Topping Station

Pick your fave toppings and sprinkle over the sauce. Here are some suggestions —
- ☑ Cheese
- ☐ Sweet peppers
- ☐ Sweetcorn
- ☐ Ham
- ☐ Pineapple
- ☐ Pepperoni slices
- ☐ Chicken
- ☐ Tuna
- ☐ Olives
- ☐ Extra veggies — tomatoes, onions, courgette slices

Take care with the hot oven!

Bake the pizza at 220°C for around 15 minutes — the crust should be golden and the cheese bubbly on top. Yum!

SPARKLING ANGEL COOKIES!

Marigold loves to make angel cookies for Dolphin and Star. Now you can make them too!

You'll Need:
- Cookie dough
- Heart shaped cutter
- 8cm round cookie cutter
- Icing tubes — we used sparkly glitter gel icing
- Sprinkles for decorating
- Garlic press

Make Cookie Dough
- 250g softened butter or margarine
- 140g icing sugar
- 1 egg
- 1 teaspoon vanilla essence
- 375g plain flour

WHAT TO DO:

1 Beat the butter and sugar together until pale coloured and fluffy.

2 Separate the egg yolk from the white. Stir the yolk only and the vanilla essence into the butter mix. Keep the egg white for later.

3 Mix in the flour. Use your hands to bring everything together into a soft dough.

4 Knead lightly till smooth then wrap in cling film and chill in the fridge for at least 30 minutes.

5 Roll out the dough on a floured board till it's about ½ cm thick.

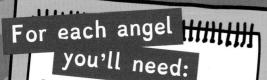

For each angle you'll need:

- 1 heart-shaped cut-out
- 1 circle cut-out
- 2 small balls of cookie dough

- Egg white (beat lightly with a fork first)

1

Place the heart on your baking sheet. This is for the wings. Brush a little of the egg white on top. Carefully fold over two edges of the dough circle like this.

TIP! The dough for the circles should be very soft so you can fold it without cracking. Knead it gently before cutting them out.

2

Lightly press the folded circle on to the heart like this. Flatten out one little ball for the head and stick it on top of the heart. Brush egg white round the top of the head.

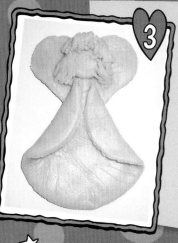

3

Squish the other dough ball through a very clean garlic press. Carefully arrange the strands for your angel's hair. Now follow the baking instructions!

DECORATE! Now add icing and sprinkles to finish off your gorgeous biscuits!

BAKE IT!

Ask an adult to help with the oven!

- Cook in an oven heated to 190°C/375°F/gas mark 5 for 10–15 minutes.

- The cookies should be very pale gold — don't let them get too dark.

- They will be soft and harden as they cool — leave until completely cold before decorating.

TOTALLY MAGIC Banana Ice

When is ice cream not ice cream? When it's bananas!

You'll Need:

☆ 4 ripe bananas

☆ Food processor or blender

Dairy and sugar free!

1

Slice the bananas, pop them in a freezer bag and freeze overnight.

Make it chocolate flavoured!

WHY NOT?

Just add 2 tablespoons of Nutella and 2 teaspoons of cocoa powder to the banana granules before you blitz it smooth!

Cream!

Tip!
Re-freeze the banana ice cream for 1–2 hours if you want a firmer texture.

2
When they're solid, ask an adult to pulse them in a food processor or blender. First, they'll turn into little banana granules.

3
Keep whizzing till they're thick and creamy like this – now you have ready-to-serve soft scoop banana ice cream!

Topping Stop!

☐ chopped nuts
☐ chocolate sauce
☐ fruit sauce
☐ mini sugar beans
☐ crushed cookies
☐ choc chips
☐ sprinkles
☐ wafers
☐ finger biscuits

YUM!

Cupcake Creation Station

Customise your cupcakes with our amazing tips!

Beautiful Buttercream

Beat 140g of butter in a bowl until soft and sift in 280g of icing sugar a little at a time, beating until smooth. Pop in an icing bag and swirl it over cupcakes!

Chocolate Nut

Add cocoa powder and a spoonful of peanut butter to the icing. Top with chopped candy bars and sweets, plus a drizzle of chocolate sauce.

Flower Power

Add a few drops of rose water to the icing and swirl over the cupcakes. Top with a sugarpaste rose and pink icing crystals.

Mint Choc Chip

Add a few drops of peppermint extract and green food colouring to the icing! Sprinkle over chocolate chips to finish!

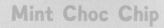

Ice Cream Sundae

Mix a few drops of vanilla essence to the buttercream and pipe on in dollops. Cover with chocolate sauce, sprinkles and a cherry on top!

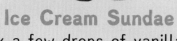

Rainbow Swirl

Separate the icing into bowls and add a few drops of food colouring to each. Spoon the colours into a piping bag and slowly pipe on a swirl. The colours will come out rainbow!

Create A Cupcake!

Design your own cute cupcake!

What ingredients will you add to make it oh-so-delicious?

Practise your decorating style here, then get baking!

I'll help you be a better baker!

BISCUIT'S BAKING TIPS!

1. Baking is science! Take the time to carefully weigh all your ingredients — this is where most things go wrong.

2. Don't be tempted to keep opening the oven to check the cakes — it makes them sink or cook unevenly!

3. Popping your cut out cookies into the fridge for 30 minutes before baking helps them better keep their shapes.

4. Start cake-baking with room temperature ingredients — eggs too! If you forget and have a cold butter emergency, grate it into your mixture.

5. Don't add too much baking powder thinking your cakes will rise to great heights. The opposite will happen and also your cake will taste dry.

6. Always line or grease baking tins, non-stick ones too. Free stuck cakes by sitting the hot tin on a damp tea towel for a few minutes.

7. Cover your worktop with clingfilm before rolling out pastry or cookie dough. Wrap it round your rolling pin too, then bin it afterwards. Cleaning done!

8. Adding a half teaspoon of instant coffee and a pinch of cinnamon to chocolate cake mix makes it taste even more chocolaty. Yum!

9. Oh no! Is there broken shell in your cracked eggs? Wet your finger and you'll easily be able to pull it out!

10. Bake with love! It makes everything taste better. Sharing your bakes with friends and family makes your hard work worth it.

Perfectly Puzzling!

Sharpen your pencils! These puzzles and quizzes will boggle your brain!

Unscramble these letters to reveal a secret message from Jacky!

PEKE IADRGNE
EKPE GWTIINR

keep Dareeing

keep _ _ _ _ _ _ ing

The Ultimate JW Test

We asked Jacky and Nick some totally tricky book questions — take the test yourself and see if you can beat them!

IT'S YOU VS JACKY VS NICK!

No peeking at our answers!

1. True or false — in *Girls in Love*, Ellie's brother is called Marge?

2. What colour shoes does Shirley own in *Wave Me Goodbye*?

3. What are the twins called in *Double Act*?

4. In *Bad Girls*, what's Mandy's orangutan called?

5. In *Buried Alive*, where do Tim and Biscuits go on holiday?

6. In *Girls Out Late*, what time does Ellie have to be home by?

7. What job do Pearl and Jodie's parents do in *My Sister Jodie*?

8. In which book does Miss Morgan appear?

9. In *Dustbin Baby*, April runs away on which birthday?

10. Who works for Happy Homes?

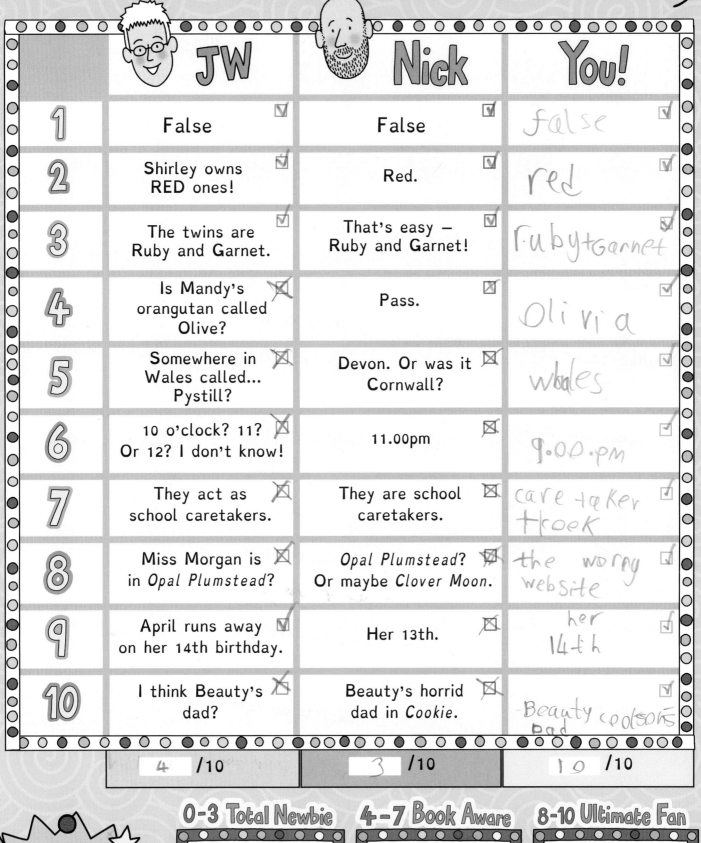

	JW	Nick	You!
1	False ☑	False ☑	false ☑
2	Shirley owns RED ones! ☑	Red. ☑	red ☑
3	The twins are Ruby and Garnet. ☑	That's easy – Ruby and Garnet! ☑	ruby+Garnet ☑
4	Is Mandy's orangutan called Olive? ☒	Pass. ☒	Olivia ☑
5	Somewhere in Wales called... Pystill? ☒	Devon. Or was it Cornwall? ☒	whales ☑
6	10 o'clock? 11? Or 12? I don't know! ☒	11.00pm ☒	9.00.pm ☑
7	They act as school caretakers. ☒	They are school caretakers. ☒	care taker trook ☑
8	Miss Morgan is in *Opal Plumstead*? ☒	*Opal Plumstead*? Or maybe *Clover Moon*. ☒	the worry website ☑
9	April runs away on her 14th birthday. ☑	Her 13th. ☒	her 14th ☑
10	I think Beauty's dad? ☒	Beauty's horrid dad in *Cookie*. ☒	Beauty cooksons pad ☑

| 4 /10 | 3 /10 | 10 /10 |

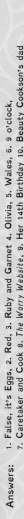

Answers: 1. False, it's Eggs, 2. Red, 3. Ruby and Garnet 4. Olivia, 5. Wales, 6. 9 o'clock, 7. Caretaker and Cook 8. *The Worry Website*, 9. Her 14th Birthday 10. Beauty Cookson's dad

THE ULTIMATE CHAMPION IS ... Me

0-3 Total Newbie
Sounds like you might be new to the JW world – don't worry, that just means you've got loads of fun reading ahead of you! We're jealous!

4-7 Book Aware
You know your JW stuff pretty well, but there's always room for improvement! Re-read the older books and you'll score higher next time!

8-10 Ultimate Fan
Success! You know almost everything there is to know about the books! Are you actually Jacqueline Wilson, by any chance?

WHO'S THE SECRET SENDER?

Who would send Justine face-like-a-pug Littlewood a Valentine's Day card? Solve the puzzles to find out!

Put the letters in the ANSWER boxes!

Poem Prank!

Oops — Tracy got a hold of Justine's card and changed the poem inside! Unscramble the highlighted letters to reveal who's NOT the secret admirer!

Roses are red
Violets are blue
Sugar is sweet
~~And so are you~~
BUT YOU LOOK LIKE POO!

Put the 1st letter in the 10th box and the 4th letter in the 9th box

Chore Challenge!

Tracy got caught teasing Justine about her card. What's her punishment? Solve this secret code to find out!

A B C D E F G H I
J K L M N O P Q R
S T U V W X Y Z

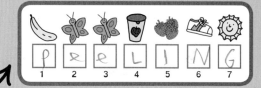

P R E L I N G
1 2 3 4 5 6 7

P O T A T O E S
8 9 10 11 12 13 14 15

Put the 2nd letter in the 6th box and the 4th letter in the 2nd box. Put the 11th letter in the 11th box.

Cam to the Rescue!

Cam buys Tracy a treat to cheer her up.
Solve the riddle to see what she gets!

My first is in call, but not in ball,
My second is the first in heart.
My third is brown, but not in brawn,
My fourth is the first in cringe.
My fifth is the second in bow.
My sixth is in love, but not in dove,
My seventh is the last in pizza.
My eighth is in tale, but not in bale,
My last is the beginning of end.

c h o c o l a t e
1 2 3 4 5 6 7 8 9

Put the 2nd letter in the 8th box, the 7th letter in the 3rd box and the last letter in the 1st box.

Valentine's Day Out!

Mike takes everyone out for a trip! Where do they go?
Fill in a letter to make two new words, then read down to find the answer!

COMI	c	HART
KIW	i	GLOO
QUEE	h	ICE
PRIZ	e	XAM
FAR	m	IND
LAV	a	PPLE

Put the 2nd letter in the 12th box and the 3rd letter in the 5th box.

Storm Scare!

There was a storm the night before Valentine's Day — Tracy thinks it was a portent of DOOM (well, Justine did receive a card...). Find the words in the wordsearch, but remember, there's one missing!

RAIN ~~WIND~~ ~~STORM~~
~~THUNDER~~ ~~VIOLENT~~
~~GUST~~ LIGHTNING
~~NIGHTMARE~~ ~~GALE~~

Put the 2nd letter 4th box, the 5th letter in the 7th box and the 8th letter in the last box.

The missing word is:

L i g h t n i n g
1 2 3 4 5 6 7 8 9

```
N K S O F J N T D H
P I T B Y G V H N F
R I G N E I J U I Q
R N R H O M V H W R
C Z I L T D S D Q U
V N E A N M J E O G
X N S J R N A R Q T
T M R O T S M R S K
G A L E L P H U E X
N E M X B V G V A K
```

ANSWER:

The secret admirer is:

e l a i n e
1 2 3 4 5 6

t h e p a i n
7 8 9 10 11 12 13

LIZZIE'S

What's Your Creative Craft?

Follow the arrows to pick a new hobby!

START Chatterbox OR Shy?

Chatty → Sweets OR Crisps?

Sweets → Hetty Feather? OR Cookie?

Shy → Bunnies OR Hamsters?

Crisps → Cosy scarf OR Book bag?

Hetty Feather

Cookie → Stars OR Hearts?

Scarf → Bunnies OR Hamsters?

Cosy scarf OR Book bag?

Stars OR Hearts?

Bunnies · Hamsters · Book bag · Hearts · Stars

Knitting
Just like Lizzie you could make cuddly knitted things to snuggle up to.

Stitching
Creating and customising with a needle and thread like Hetty is so you!

Baking
Like Beauty, you'd love to produce yummy cookies and cakes for your besties!

Are You Zipmouth or Loudmouth?

- ☒ I've told a secret to make me more popular at school
- ☒ I've told a secret by accident – it slipped out!
- ☒ I don't join in with gossip about others in school
- ☒ I often get told off for chatting
- ☒ I wouldn't tell my BF if her new top didn't suit her
- ☒ I never snoop at my birthday or Christmas prezzies
- ☒ I've been banned from using the phone!
- ☒ I like to read my mum's TV mag

QUIZZES

Tick four boxes that sound most like you then count up your score to find out!

Mostly Pink

Zipmouth

You can be totally trusted to keep a secret or surprise.

Mostly Blue

Chattermouth

Ooops! You try not to talk but sometimes you just can't stop yourself.

Mostly Green

Loudmouth

Oh my! You just can't keep quiet no matter how hard you try!

Cross Words

Can you fit these words correctly into the grid? See how quickly you can do it.

☑ ROSEHIP TEA

☑ GREAT GRAN

☑ KNITTING

☑ HOSPITAL

☑ DOLLS   ☑ LIZZIE   ☑ SAM

☑ JAKE   ☐ PIZZA   ☑ RORY

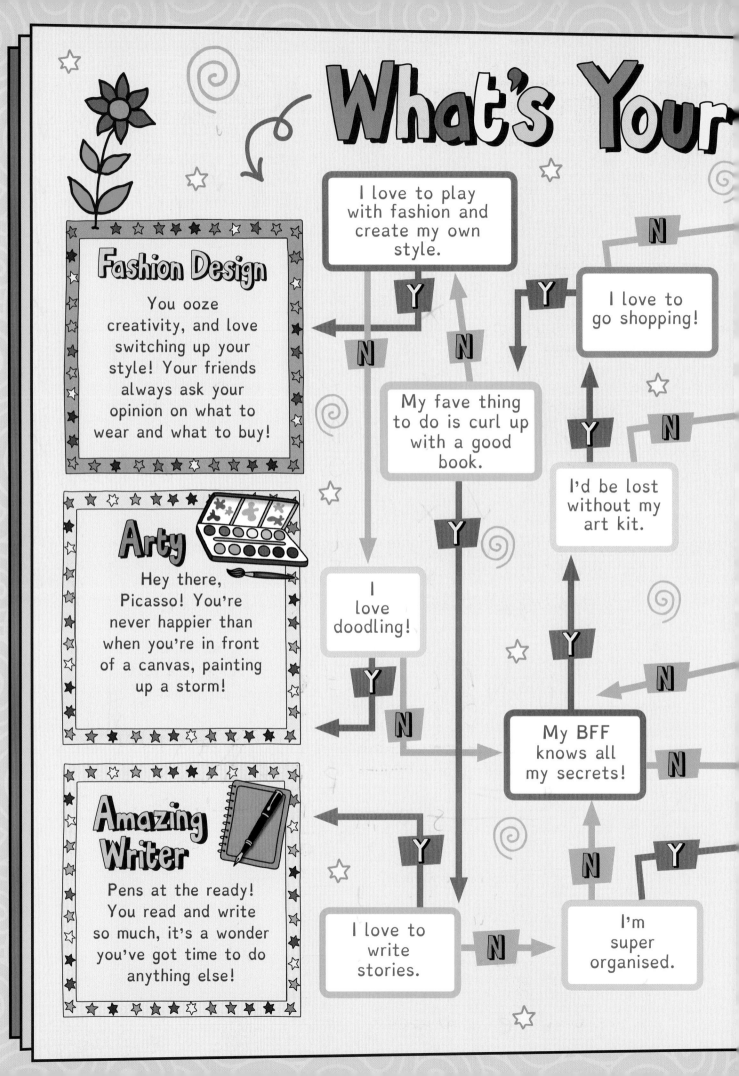

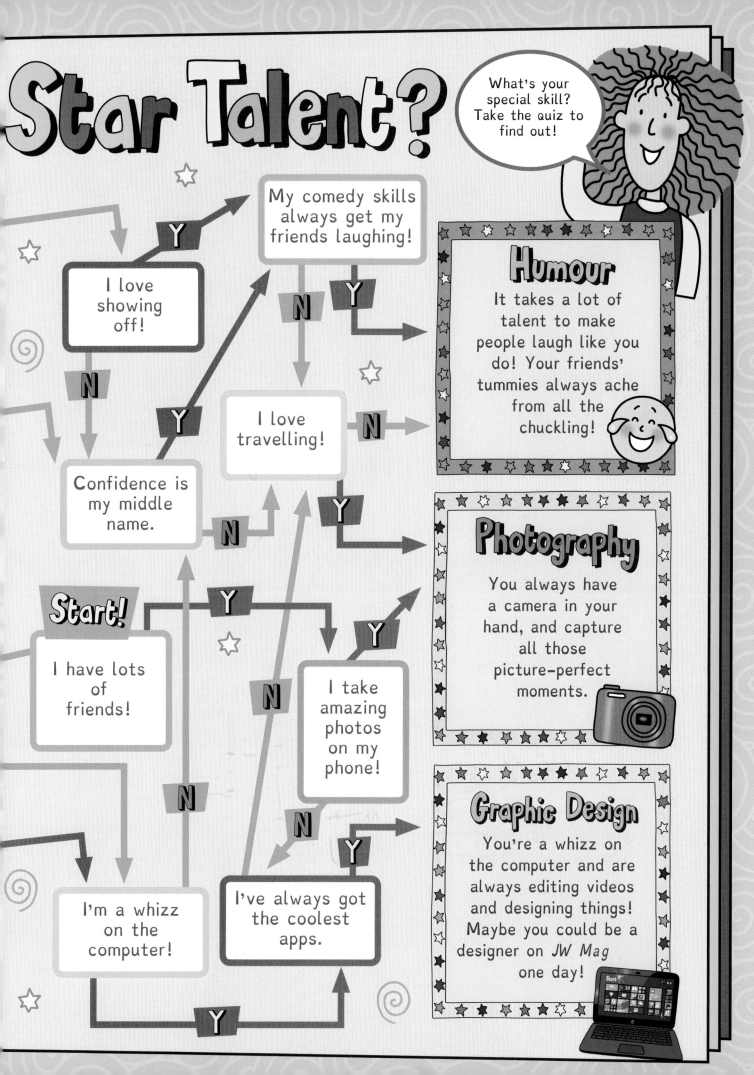

You Know You're a JW Fan when...

You can name who these belong to!

1 Marigold

2 Mellisa

3 shirley

4 india

The Diary of ANNE FRANK

Answers:
1. Marigold from *The Illustrated Mum*, 2. Melissa from *The Worst Thing About My Sister*, 3. Shirley's from *Wave me Goodbye*, 4. India from *Secrets*

You ace this JW pop quiz!

1. What is Tilly's old teddy bear called in *Rent a Bridesmaid*?

2. Where do Rose Rivers' grandparents live?

3. What is Katie's nasty nickname for Andy in *The Suitcase Kid*?

4. Who shares a birthday with Tracy Beaker?

5. What is the name of Marty's big sister?

6. What team is Tim part of in *Cliffhanger*?

You've done all of these things...

- ☐ Learned all the words to *The Jackie Jackie Song*!
- ☐ Used a birthday wish for a brand new JW story!
- ☐ Finished ALL the JW books at your library!
- ☐ You re-read your fave JW book every year!

You can spot the fib!

1. Jacky owns over 20,000 books!
2. Nick has illustrated every book written by Jacky!
3. Jacky is a BAFTA winner!
4. Nick sold his first picture when he was nine!

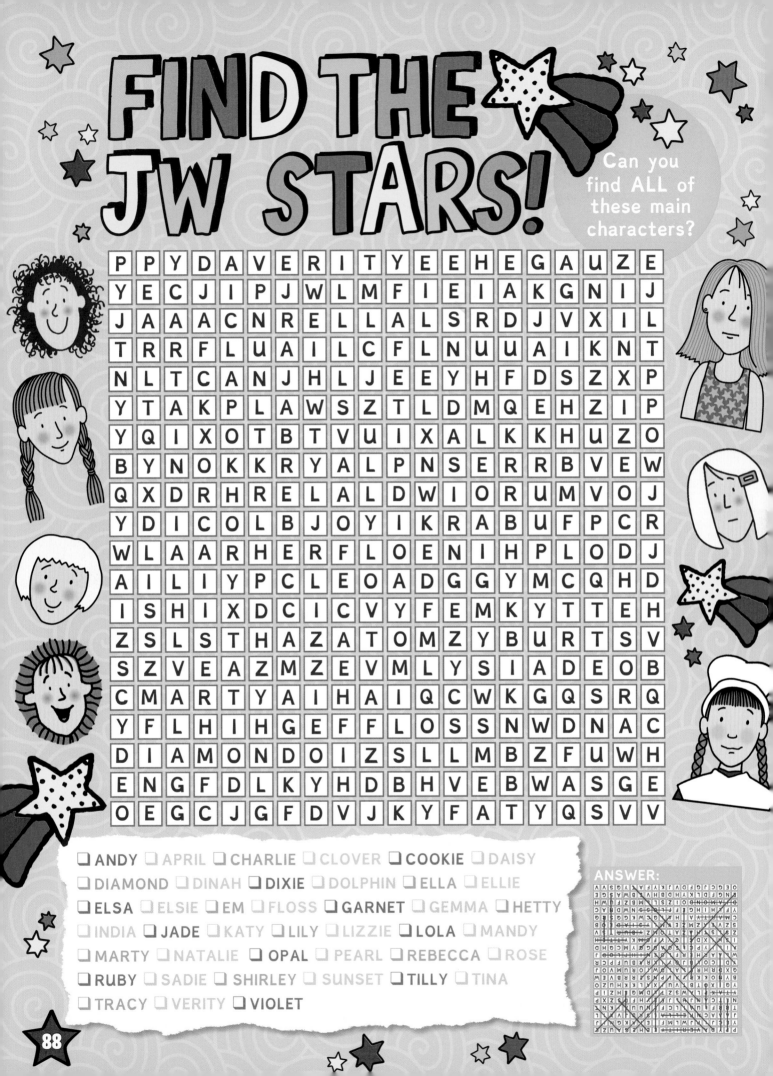

FIND THE JW STARS!

Can you find ALL of these main characters?

P	P	Y	D	A	V	E	R	I	T	Y	E	E	H	E	G	A	U	Z	E
Y	E	C	J	I	P	J	W	L	M	F	I	E	I	A	K	G	N	I	J
J	A	A	A	C	N	R	E	L	L	A	L	S	R	D	J	V	X	I	L
T	R	R	F	L	U	A	I	L	C	F	L	N	U	U	A	I	K	N	T
N	L	T	C	A	N	J	H	L	J	E	E	Y	H	F	D	S	Z	X	P
Y	T	A	K	P	L	A	W	S	Z	T	L	D	M	Q	E	H	Z	I	P
Y	Q	I	X	O	T	B	T	V	U	I	X	A	L	K	K	H	U	Z	O
B	Y	N	O	K	K	R	Y	A	L	P	N	S	E	R	R	B	V	E	W
Q	X	D	R	H	R	E	L	A	L	D	W	I	O	R	U	M	V	O	J
Y	D	I	C	O	L	B	J	O	Y	I	K	R	A	B	U	F	P	C	R
W	L	A	A	R	H	E	R	F	L	O	E	N	I	H	P	L	O	D	J
A	I	L	I	Y	P	C	L	E	O	A	D	G	G	Y	M	C	Q	H	D
I	S	H	I	X	D	C	I	C	V	Y	F	E	M	K	Y	T	T	E	H
Z	S	L	S	T	H	A	Z	A	T	O	M	Z	Y	B	U	R	T	S	V
S	Z	V	E	A	Z	M	Z	E	V	M	L	Y	S	I	A	D	E	O	B
C	M	A	R	T	Y	A	I	H	A	I	Q	C	W	K	G	Q	S	R	Q
Y	F	L	H	I	H	G	E	F	F	L	O	S	S	N	W	D	N	A	C
D	I	A	M	O	N	D	O	I	Z	S	L	L	M	B	Z	F	U	W	H
E	N	G	F	D	L	K	Y	H	D	B	H	V	E	B	W	A	S	G	E
O	E	G	C	J	G	F	D	V	J	K	Y	F	A	T	Y	Q	S	V	V

☐ ANDY ☐ APRIL ☐ CHARLIE ☐ CLOVER ☐ COOKIE ☐ DAISY
☐ DIAMOND ☐ DINAH ☐ DIXIE ☐ DOLPHIN ☐ ELLA ☐ ELLIE
☐ ELSA ☐ ELSIE ☐ EM ☐ FLOSS ☐ GARNET ☐ GEMMA ☐ HETTY
☐ INDIA ☐ JADE ☐ KATY ☐ LILY ☐ LIZZIE ☐ LOLA ☐ MANDY
☐ MARTY ☐ NATALIE ☐ OPAL ☐ PEARL ☐ REBECCA ☐ ROSE
☐ RUBY ☐ SADIE ☐ SHIRLEY ☐ SUNSET ☐ TILLY ☐ TINA
☐ TRACY ☐ VERITY ☐ VIOLET

ANSWER:

88

Use these cutouts to decorate your pen pots on page 22!

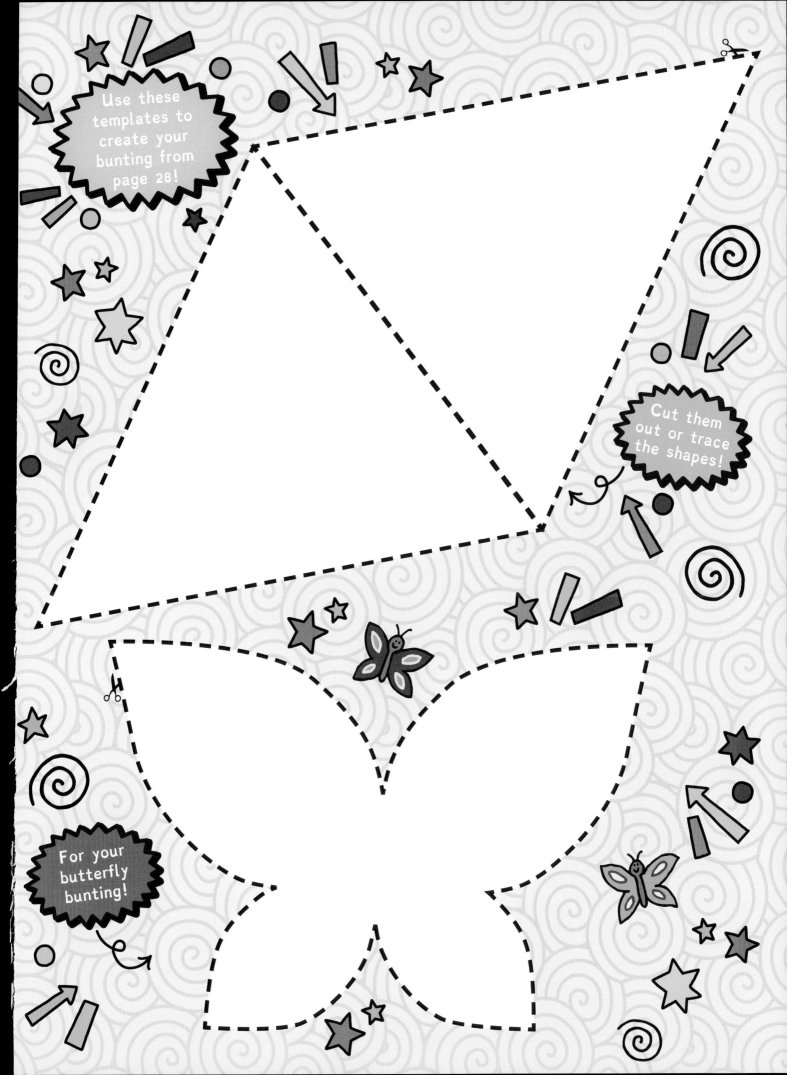

Use these templates to create your bunting from page 28!

Cut them out or trace the shapes!

For your butterfly bunting!

A Year of Epic

Never be stuck with story starters for every week of the year – tick them off as you complete each one!

27. Write about a time you were mega embarrassed. Turn your blushes into a lol-tastic tale.

28. You've invented something amazing! What is it? Will it save lives, or make you lots of money?

29. Write a review of a book you didn't enjoy. What are the reasons?

30. Wow! You wake up and you're Jacky! Describe your life as a top author.

32. The worst thing about being me is...

33. Choose a random part of a text conversation from your phone. Write a story based on the texts.

34. What would you put in a time capsule to be opened in the year 3000? Write your list and your reasons for choosing them.

36. 'The vase wobbled on the edge of the table then fell with a crash.' What happens next?

37. Every day you pass a door that's always closed and locked. Then one day the door is open. You step inside and...

38. Write about a super-hero whose life has been spoiled by their special powers.

39. Try writing a song about something you did or felt today.

42. Imagine you're the person who opens the time capsule in the year 3000. What do you think of the things inside? Do you even know what they are?

43. Oopsie! You drank a witch's potion. What happens to you?

44. Would you rather have elastic arms or hair that grows at lightning speed? Write about your strange life.

47. What school means to me... Love it or hate it, we all have an opinion. Write about it!

48. Describe your favourite meal. Make it sound so delicious that anyone would be tempted by it.

49. If you could live anywhere in the world, where would you choose and why?

50. Write about a goal you've set for yourself and why you want to achieve it.